THE DEAD BOY

Joe Pintauro

BROADWAY PLAY PUBLISHING INC
New York
www.broadwayplaypublishing.com
info@broadwayplaypublishing.com

THE DEAD BOY
© Copyright 2005 Joe Pintauro

Cover art from New Jersey Repertory Company production

First published by B P P I in *Plays By Joe Pintauro: Full Length Plays* in July 2005
This edition: March 2019
I S B N: 978-0-88145-805-3

Book design: Marie Donovan
Page make-up: Adobe InDesign
Typeface: Palatino

This version of THE DEAD BOY, in slightly different form, was presented at the Royal Court under Stephen Daldry in the year 1991. Directed by Ken Butler.

It was a selection of the Eugene O'Neill Conference in 1999 (Casey Childs, Director). Subsequent productions took place at The Actors Theater, Los Angeles (Jack Heller Producer/Director), The Royal Court (Sean Mathias, Director), and Saratoga Stages (Jack Hofsiss, Director).

THE DEAD BOY was produced at New Jersey Repertory Company (Artistic Director: SuzAnne Barabas; Executive Producer: Gabor Barabas) in Long Branch from 3 May-9 June 2002. The cast and creative contributor were:

CARDINAL HAMILTON ....Leonard Auclair
FATHER ANGELO ROSETTI............................ Burt Edwards
FATHER ROBERT SHERIDAN .... Anthony Newfield
TONY MCGUIRE ....Ken Wiesinger
WILL DRAPER/YOUNG PRIEST ....Cary Woodworth

Director .... William Martin

A workshop presentation in January 2004 took place at the San Carlos Opera House in Key West (Mare Contrare, Artistic Director) The cast and creative contributor were:

FATHER ANDREW DAVIS.................................Denis Parlato
FATHER ANGELO ROSETTI...........................Richard Grusin
FRANCIS CARDINAL HAMILTON....................Roy Scheider
KATHERINE MCGUIRE...............................Mercedes Ruehl
WILL DRAPER/THE YOUNG PRIEST.......Cary Woodworth

Director..Jay Ranelli

CHARACTERS

FATHER ANDREW DAVIS, *49*
FATHER ANGELO ROSETTI, *70*
FRANCIS CARDINAL HAMILTON, *60*
KATHERINE MCGUIRE, *30-40*
WILL DRAPER/THE YOUNG PRIEST, *20-25*

THE YOUNG PRIEST *is* FATHER DAVIS *as a young man and can be seen by no one on stage except* FATHER DAVIS. WILL DRAPER, *on the other hand, is a male prostitute who is all too real. In the mind of* FATHER DAVIS, WILL DRAPER *and* THE YOUNG PRIEST *are one and the same. That is why, here, both characters are played by the same actor.*

SETTING

A circular arcade of Gothic arches, usually the side altars of a cathedral, here simply resembling empty spaces as seen through the lower invisible exterior walls of a Cathedral. This Cathedral has an open roof casting daylight down to the middle of the set, or sanctuary, where there sits an elaborate Cathedra, or Cardinal's throne. This great chair may come downstage through the arches.

The word Cathedra existed before the word, Cathedral. It is the presence of this seat, that makes any church to be called a Cathedral. As the Gothic arcade turns carousel like, other locations become visible, a cafe, a rectory dining room and priests' quarters.

The time is the present.

Scene One

(Saturday. Nine P M. Inside the Cathedral. A single Cathedral bell rings nine times. FATHER DAVIS *and the* YOUNG PRIEST, *enter from left and right stage having just completed saying mass. They put down their chalices and begin to divest themselves of their heavy vestments. The older priest,* FATHER DAVIS *is at stage left, the* YOUNG PRIEST, *stage right. Their movements are like mirror images, each priest removing each part of their costumes at the same moment, until the younger priest notices and attempts to disrupt the timing while* FATHER DAVIS, *taunts him by matching his actions.)*

(When they are undressed down to their black Roman cassocks, their normal dress, ROSETTI *enters, carrying a cup of coffee with a saucer on top of it. On the saucer is a croissant. He speaks to* FATHER DAVIS *completely unaware of the* YOUNG PRIEST's *presence.)*

ROSETTI: We've got problems. The Cardinal wants you to join him for breakfast.

FATHER DAVIS: What's that?

ROSETTI: I sneaked it out of the kitchen.

FATHER DAVIS: You want me to eat breakfast here in the sacristy?

ROSETTI: There's someone up there with him. They're setting you up for an intervention.

FATHER DAVIS: What do you want me to do?

ROSETTI: I don't know. I have to think. Have your coffee. I'll have to make something up.

FATHER DAVIS: Don't get into trouble.

ROSETTI: You're the one who's in the trouble. That sounded selfish. You know I feel for you.

FATHER DAVIS: What are they saying?

ROSETTI: No mention of the kid or any of that, but the thing is, it's not just any reporter.

FATHER DAVIS: Who is he?

ROSETTI: She. Katie McGuire.

FATHER DAVIS: She's happily married in California.

ROSETTI: Not any more. Rothenberg hired her to come back here and write for the paper.

FATHER DAVIS: That's a rather strange coincidence.

ROSETTI: Smells like another one of the Cardinal's ideas.

FATHER DAVIS: If he's trying to get her to help me he'd be better off with the devil himself. You say she's in the rectory right now?

ROSETTI: Eating salmon, bagels and scrambled eggs. I should know. I scrambled them.

FATHER DAVIS: I guess you're right. Now how are you going to say you didn't see me? Where could I have slipped out to?

ROSETTI: I'm getting a little tired of lying for you.

FATHER DAVIS: Is that croissant for me?

ROSETTI: Oh. Stay down here. You hear me? Don't move till I come back. I'll be back down as soon as they let me.

(ROSETTI *exits.* FATHER DAVIS *salutes the* YOUNG PRIEST *with his cup and makes a gesture of offering a bite of the croissant. He gets a rather sober refusal.* FATHER DAVIS *starts eating his breakfast.)*

(ROSETTI *enters the space where the* CARDINAL *and* KATHERINE MCGUIRE *are dining and offers coffee to* KATHERINE *who refuses it, but he pours more coffee into the* CARDINAL'*s cup.)*

CARDINAL: Ah Father Rosetti. Come here and talk to us. The Cathedral all locked up?

ROSETTI: Not yet, Frank.

CARDINAL: I don't want it open all day.

ROSETTI: There are people still sitting around after Mass.

CARDINAL: What mass? There's no other mass.

ROSETTI: The visiting priest…he said Mass at one of the side altars.

CARDINAL: There's no visiting priest. Oh, that visiting priest. He said Mass? Thank God. That's a good sign. Good. Good. Well get him up here.

KATHERINE: What's going on?

CARDINAL: Oh forgive me, Angelo. Do you remember Anthony McGuire, Grand Knight of the Knights of Columbus? Well this is his…

ROSETTI: I baptized Katie under your predecessor Cardinal, Cardinal…Cardinal…

CARDINAL: Cardinal…

ROSETTI: The one before you.

CARDINAL: Of course, uh. Cardinal…

CARDINAL/ROSETTI: Later.

ROSETTI: Your father was a layman of low rank in this rectory but of the highest order anywhere in this human world.

KATHERINE: You honor my Dad, I honor you.

CARDINAL: Father Rosetti loves to make it known how he pre-dates me at the Cathedral. He was Confessor to Cardinal... what's his name and apparently his job goes with the territory so now the good father confesses me and all the Cathedral clergly, including the nuns, so he knows far too much about everything around here. And he's the Reverend exorcist of the diocese.

KATHERINE: *(Overlap)* I know.

ROSETTI: *(Overlap)* Frank, don't make light...

CARDINAL: You can smell the sweat of the saints who have brushed past his cassock, both real and false saints, and, beware, devils. As if exorcist were not burden enough, he's Master of Ceremonies, cook, sacristan while I'm a mere prince of the church, one step below the Pope but Father Rosetti resides in the lofty literary realms of say...Quasimodo? There's a bit of the bell ringer in the good father.

ROSETTI: Let's not be rude to your guest.

CARDINAL: Have I been rude, Katie?

ROSETTI: She wouldn't tell you.

CARDINAL: Oh he's on your case now. How would you like it if I had her preach to the people? How's about it Katherine? We'll make you a lector.

ROSETTI: *(Aside)* Frank, you're showing off.

CARDINAL: *(Aside)* I'm trying to be entertaining.

ROSETTI: *(Aside)* It isn't working.

KATHERINE: Forget Lector. Make me a priest. Something a woman could sink her teeth into.

CARDINAL: You're not even a member of the faith anymore.

KATHERINE: Who told you that?

CARDINAL: By the way, women were not among the twelve apostles.

KATHERINE: Oh, we only get to wash your feet? Well I don't do feet. How about the order of exorcist? I'd put that to good use.

CARDINAL: I dare say you already possess those powers.

KATHERINE: Don't let me come between you two. I'm sorry not to meet your "Visiting Priest" Maybe I'll catch him next time. If he "visits" again.

CARDINAL: Stay where you are, please. I agree with Angelo about your father. A glorious Irishman who'd have made the perfect priest we all dream about. The good ones always get away.

KATHERINE: I'm glad Dad left the seminary or I'd not have been born, although with the way things are today…

CARDINAL: Marriage is a kind of priesthood too. Both have irreversible vows. Something you forgot.

KATHERINE: Divorce is like catching the flu, Eminence. Even though you get the shot, it can still happen to you.

CARDINAL: Please go lock up the church now, Father. And have whatever priest you can find down there, join us for breakfast.

(ROSETTI *exits*.)

CARDINAL: Your mother begged me to beg you to let her see her grand daughter.

KATHERINE: Have her call my ex-husband's lawyer.

CARDINAL: Poor Katie. On the outs with everyone.

KATHERINE: Buddha still loves me.

CARDINAL: And Buddha loved Jesus. Why can't you?

KATHERINE: I can. Of course I can. God. I...I know what you want. You have ethics and I have ethics and they are not similar but we have them anyway and I can't help you out with Father Davis.

CARDINAL: You loved him.

KATHERINE: I hardly knew him.

CARDINAL: I meant as a friend. I...

KATHERINE: He was never a friend.

CARDINAL: I know you have to say that.

KATHERINE: I don't have to say anything.

CARDINAL: You used to follow him around here like a love sick puppy.

KATHERINE: I really have to go now.

CARDINAL: He returns more missing kids to their families than the F B I. He practically wiped out prostitution, something no mayor has yet to do. He set up the biggest shelter for homeless kids in the world. He carries a gun and not just to go to the bank. He has enough enemies. He doesn't need people like us to join their ranks.

KATHERINE: What if he's a criminal?

CARDINAL: People are made of love and hate. Guilty or innocent they will hate priests. This is centuries old. But giving up on the faith you were born in, what's with you?

KATHERINE: Some of us re-invent ourselves to survive.

CARDINAL: Re-invent. Malarkey. Some of us make commitments and stick by them all our lives.

KATHERINE: Okay. One day Cardinal, I said to myself, over here is Buddha, serene, even asleep, like God, like nature. But over here...is this near naked man nailed to a cross. And he scares me and touches me. You have to admit it's a pretty awesome display of violence. Then my daughter was born and I thought, little girls wear him around their necks for first holy communion. A dying God for every little girl.

CARDINAL: God will never die.

KATHERINE: Ask Father Davis and he'll tell you God is dead.

CARDINAL: I will ask him. He'll be up here any minute. We can both ask him.

KATHERINE: I'm sure Father Rosetti warned him of the trap you set for him.

CARDINAL: He lives here, eats here.

KATHERINE: I thought he lived at Rescue House.

CARDINAL: Too dangerous for him to sleep in that awful building, fortunately, or I'd be stuck in this rectory day and night with Father Rosetti.

KATHERINE: I'm not the ideal person for this assignment.

CARDINAL: Then ask Rothenberg to take you off it. Simple.

KATHERINE: My problem is, I spoke to the kid. If you'd spoken to him you'd feel the same.

CARDINAL: How do you feel?

KATHERINE: Sick to my stomach. Where is my coat?

(Freeze. Lights on the sacristy. The YOUNG PRIEST comes closer to FATHER DAVIS who has finished his coffee and has started to leave.)

Scene Two

YOUNG PRIEST: Don't leave. Where do I go? Do I stay here?

FATHER DAVIS: The Cardinal's paranoid about locking the Cathedral. Makes the place cold as a morgue.

YOUNG PRIEST: I don't mind the cold.

FATHER DAVIS: Then stay here. But my feet are freezing and I'm going to my room.

YOUNG PRIEST: When I was a kid, I loved how cool it was in church, the cold stone, the blue light, Easter lilies, white linens. Those Madonna lilies. The perfume…almost the breath of angels.

FATHER DAVIS: Where did you come from?

YOUNG PRIEST: Saint Theresa's parish. Spanish…

FATHER DAVIS: Pilar Ortiz.

YOUNG PRIEST: You know the parish? Yeah. Pilar Ortiz. I got there this morning… and her daughter…

FATHER DAVIS: Serena.

YOUNG PRIEST: Yeah. She says, "my mother's in a coma". So I whisper in the old woman's ear: *"El Padre esta' aqui Señora. Yo soy el Padre."* The old lady opens her mouth for the host. Swallows the Sacrament and starts talking. "Father…I get to heaven.

YOUNG PRIEST/FATHER DAVIS: My first Ave Maria, I say for you."

YOUNG PRIEST: She must've died the minute I left because…

FATHER DAVIS: The funeral's posted in the sacristy.

(The YOUNG PRIEST *smiles, confused by how* FATHER DAVIS *knows these things.)*

YOUNG PRIEST: Yeah. To think that beautiful old lady's in heaven right now, praying for me! I'm so…God, I could shatter. I…

FATHER DAVIS: I never realized how dangerously romantic you were.

YOUNG PRIEST: That is cruel.

FATHER DAVIS: C'mere. See that bridge? Two auto deaths a week on that exit ramp. Some old guy drops dead in the tenements. His fluids are staining the ceiling below and the cops call you to give the last rites to a stinking pile of flesh.

YOUNG PRIEST: That's our life.

FATHER DAVIS: Oh, it can break your heart.

YOUNG PRIEST: Only God could break my heart.

FATHER DAVIS: He will.

YOUNG PRIEST: What? You should be giving good example…not scandalizing…a younger priest.

FATHER DAVIS: You're the only thing I give a damn about.

YOUNG PRIEST: I don't want to know you. Don't want you to talk to me.

FATHER DAVIS: Then stop stalking me.

(FATHER DAVIS *exits. The* YOUNG PRIEST *disappears into the Cathedral shadows.*)

Scene Three

(ROSETTI *stealthily returns to the Rectory dining room with* KATHERINE's *coat. He taps the* CARDINAL. *Unfreeze*)

CARDINAL: Rosetti! You nearly gave me a heart attack. Where is he?

ROSETTI: Calm down, Frank.

CARDINAL: Telling a calm person to calm down is
the most counter productive command on earth. Do
not call me Frank in front of people and in lieu of
appearing out of nowhere, knock.

ROSETTI: There's no door, Eminence.

CARDINAL: Here. I make you a gift of the dinner bell.
Ring it when you approach.

(KATHERINE *is putting on her coat.*)

CARDINAL: Hold it there McGuire.

ROSETTI: *(Ringing the bell)* Leper approaching! A young
man is sitting in your chair.

CARDINAL: What chair?

ROSETTI: The Cathedra in the Cathedral sanctuary, your
Eminence. I can't lock up because he refuses to move.

CARDINAL: Where's Father Davis?

ROSETTI: No where that I am able to say.

CARDINAL: Another mental reservation? Call the police.

ROSETTI: And tell them a person needs to go to
confession as a matter of life and death and the
Cardinal wants to kick him out of church.

CARDINAL: Why can't you hear him?

ROSETTI: I offered. He's demanding you!

CARDINAL: People demand Barbara Streisand and
Michael Jordan. Do they get them? No.

ROSETTI: I'm not fond of how you just…

CARDINAL: Apply for a transfer.

ROSETTI: I hereby apply.

CARDINAL: Request denied. Take care of it, Angelo.

(ROSETTI *rings the bell again.*)

KATHERINE: The leper.

ROSETTI: Seriously, Frank. He's waiting down there for you. He doesn't want me.

CARDINAL: What would you do if I were in Rome?

ROSETTI: I would watch T V and drink tea from dawn till dusk with scones and clotted cream.

CARDINAL: This is the sort of thing I get day after day.

ROSETTI: He says it's a matter of life and death. He doesn't appear to be kidding.

(Hands him a confessional stole)

CARDINAL: Get her more coffee.

KATHERINE: I couldn't. It was lovely.

CARDINAL: I gave my life to this church Katie like your father and like you I thought.

KATHERINE: I don't want to be hurt.

CARDINAL: Neither do I. I'm so scared. My Mass ends at noon. Angie, make sure Father Davis shows up this time.

ROSETTI: He'll be wanting to talk to you first. I suggest Ms McGuire arrive at twelve-thirty.

CARDINAL: Talk to me what about?

ROSETTI: It is not for me to say.

CARDINAL: I'm not asking you to break the seal. If I were, I'd be asking WHY HE STOPPED SAYING MASS until this morning.

ROSETTI: Who's side are you on?

(ROSETTI turns his back to the CARDINAL and starts walking off.)

CARDINAL: I WOULD DIE ON THE CROSS FOR HIM AND YOU KNOW IT. God help me. *(He exits.)*

KATHERINE: Why is he bothering?

ROSETTI: Imagine a glob of hot red wax pressed upon the lips of a priest.

KATHERINE: Okay.

ROSETTI: That is the seal of confession. Perfect secrecy in exchange for perfect honesty.

KATHERINE: What's… What are you saying?

ROSETTI: Wouldn't I know, as confessor to these priests, the quality of their remorse for their sins?

KATHERINE: You can absolve a sin, but you can't prevent it from happening again, Father.

ROSETTI: A good journalist would try to understand the heart of a sinner. That was Shakespeare's secret.

KATHERINE: I'm not writing a play.

ROSETTI: You were missed here.

KATHERINE: By whom?

ROSETTI: Your bad priest. You want to help him? Don't show up tomorrow.

Scene Four

(*The* YOUNG PRIEST *has transformed into* WILL DRAPER.)

CARDINAL: Do you realize you're sitting on a sacred chair? The seat of the Cathedral. We're going to a confession box.

WILL: I'm claustrophobic.

CARDINAL: Oh. This matter of life and death, is it your life?

WILL: Someone else's.

CARDINAL: Then kneel here. May God who has enlightened every heart help you to know your sins and trust in his mercy.

WILL: Amen.

CARDINAL: You're Catholic?

WILL: Yes.

CARDINAL: Let's get this over with.

WILL: My sins are gonna gross you out.

CARDINAL: I've heard it all. Don't be afraid.

WILL: My Dad…

CARDINAL: Your Dad? Go on?

WILL: He usta give it me up the ass.

CARDINAL: Oh dear Jesus!

WILL: I warned you.

CARDINAL: That was his sin, not yours.

WILL: But I wanted it.

CARDINAL: No you didn't.

WILL: I'm tellin' you I wanted it. How am I gonna be forgiven? I wanted it.

CARDINAL: Number of times.

WILL: Fifteen, twenty, I dunno. Shit. (He cries.)

CARDINAL: Easy now son. Are those all your sins?

WILL: No. No. I've let everything be done to me. Sexual intercourse with women. Everything. Drugs. I'm a Dead Boy.

CARDINAL: Say again?

WILL: Dead Boy. 'Cause we hang out down the docks. No family, drugs, we get sick, so they call us already dead.

CARDINAL: You're not to call yourself that anymore. Is that clear?

WILL: Yeah. Thank you. *(Sniffling)* Got another sin. I did something bad...to a priest.

CARDINAL: What did you do? What priest?

WILL: He lives here.

CARDINAL: What did you do to him?

WILL: Lied about him to a woman from the paper.

CARDINAL: God help us.

WILL: I needed the five hundred. I didn't think she'd bring it but when she did I had to make somethin' up. Like the priest touched me and did stuff.

CARDINAL: You awful kid.

WILL: You can't call me that.

CARDINAL: You're absolutely right. I'm sorry. How old are you?

WILL: Legal age but I said it was when I was a minor. Like I said I needed the money so...

CARDINAL: So you destroyed a priest's reputation?

WILL: It's done. I wanna forget about it. It's why I'm here.

CARDINAL: But you can't just say it's done and you want to forget about it.

WILL: Are you sposta grill me like this?

CARDINAL: I'm sorry.

WILL: I came to you, remember?

CARDINAL: I'm sorry. Continue.

WILL: That's it. Those are my sins.

CARDINAL: For your penance, I want you to say one rosary.

WILL: Don't have rosary beads.

CARDINAL: Here. These were my Mothers so please return them. Now make your act of contrition and I'll meet you at the rectory door.

WILL: What did you have in mind?

CARDINAL: We'll take a taxi to the paper.

WILL: *(Overlap)* Uh uh. *(No)*

CARDINAL: Do you know what restitution is?

WILL: If it means, give back the money, I spent it.

CARDINAL: I will make you a gift of five hundred dollars in an envelope.

WILL: Ain't doin' it.

CARDINAL: You tell them the truth. You needed money and made up a story.

WILL: Don't make me.

CARDINAL: I can't give you absolution if you don't intend to do restitution. Tomorrow morning you return the money to the paper from whence it came. Do you know how to get there?

WILL: No.

CARDINAL: I'll go with you.

WILL: No.

CARDINAL: I'll give you the address and twenty dollars. You take a cab.

WILL: How do I get home?

CARDINAL: Okay. Forty dollars. You ask for Mr Rothenberg. I'll give you a letter.

WILL: Okay.

CARDINAL: Promise on my rosary beads.

WILL: I promise. *(He kisses the cross on the beads.)*

CARDINAL: Be proud of your courage. Sorry about my tone, I...

WILL: I'm used to it.

CARDINAL: Act of contrition...

WILL: Oh my God, I have sinned against you whom I love above all things. I firmly intend, to do penance and to sin no more. Our Savior Jesus Christ suffered and died for us. In his name, my God, have mercy.

Scene Five

(Later that night, ROSETTI *enters* FATHER DAVIS's *room with a box of pastries. Puts it down near a pile of opened mail then begins furiously searching through* FATHER DAVIS's *things as the priest enters. Caught in the act,* ROSETTI *picks a letter up from the floor that he dropped.)*

FATHER DAVIS: What do you want, Angelo?

ROSETTI: Ou. You scared me.

FATHER DAVIS: What's in your hand?

ROSETTI: Appears to be a letter.

FATHER DAVIS: Why don't you open it?

ROSETTI: Do I have to use this dagger?

FATHER DAVIS: Angelo, it's a letter opener. No one is going to kill himself.

*(*ROSETTI *starts slicing open the letter.)*

ROSETTI: That pimp man called claiming you abducted his fiancee.

FATHER DAVIS: She's not his girlfriend. She's his prostitute. And he cut up her face with a bottle.

ROSETTI: He wants financial recompense.

FATHER DAVIS: She's on her way home to Texas. If he comes again, call the police.

(ROSETTI *removes a check from the letter.*)

ROSETTI: A check for one thousand. (*He reads.*) I'm the mother of two, and own my own business. Ten years ago you found me tied to a bed... Oh no. Oh my God. Beautiful children.

FATHER DAVIS: What were you looking for Angie?

ROSETTI: I have to return uh...*Fatal Attraction*. Here it is! Did you enjoy it? It was based on *Madame Butterfly*.

FATHER DAVIS: You could've fooled me. What's in the box?

ROSETTI: Pastries, from Saint Theresas, from a Serena Ortiz.

(FATHER DAVIS *is moved as he tenderly opens the box. He offers one to* ROSETTI *who declines.*)

FATHER DAVIS: Bring them to the kitchen.

ROSETTI: If you want the real *Madame Butterfly*, I have the La Scala production with Yosuko Hayashi, 1986. And I have tapes of Callas in Chicago and Tebaldi at the Met in that amazing production where...

(*The* YOUNG PRIEST *appears.*)

FATHER DAVIS: Angie...

ROSETTI: ...the cherry blossoms, every individual petal came trickling down every night by the hundreds...

FATHER DAVIS: Angie, may we share opera notes another...?

ROSETTI: Of course.

(ROSETTI *is perplexed by* FATHER DAVIS' *stare into space.*)

ROSETTI: I booked you with him right after his eleven o'clock mass, so join him at breakfast and tell him

you're leaving on Monday. Yes, I'm telling you to lie
to him. Pack right now. Tonight. Leave your bag in
the sacristy. Did you hear me? And slip out before she
shows up.

(ROSETTI *exits. The* YOUNG PRIEST *angrily stares it out
with* FATHER DAVIS. *Lights grow brighter and brighter.*)

Scene Six

(*Noon Sunday. All lights in the cathedral are lit as after the
high mass. An acolyte crosses, carrying a smoking incense
pot into the sacristy. Lights on the* CARDINAL's *Office.*
FATHER DAVIS *and the* CARDINAL *are together.*)

CARDINAL: She is not the Katie McGuire you knew.
She even looks different. Ten years in California, six
at Stanford to study journalism. She got married,
divorced and she has a five year old daughter.

FATHER DAVIS: What is she doing here?

CARDINAL: I suggested to Rothenberg that he hire her.
She has no idea.

FATHER DAVIS: To what end?

CARDINAL: How was I to know they made her a
Buddhist in California? Her first day on the job
Rothenberg sends her to the crazy kid who said those
lies about you. That terrible young man.

FATHER DAVIS: You should have talked to me.

CARDINAL: By now he's gone to Rothenberg and
apologized for his prank, so you can thank the Blessed
Mother. It's over.

FATHER DAVIS: Frank, it's Sunday. Rothenberg is not
there. We have to talk before she gets here.

CARDINAL: What does Rosetti want you to tell me now?

(ROSETTI *enters carrying a breakfast tray.*)

ROSETTI: Your Eminence Ms McGuire is here. Early. I told her she must wait.

FATHER DAVIS: Don't let her in until I've had a word…

CARDINAL: You two are going to reconcile. Here she is.

(KATHERINE *enters.*)

CARDINAL: You remember Father Davis.

KATHERINE: Hello, Father.

CARDINAL: Rosetti, coffee for…

KATHERINE: Not me.

CARDINAL: I'll take it. I'm dehydrating.

(The CARDINAL *accepts the cup.)*

CARDINAL: Katherine, in the future, any matters involving my priests should come to this office first, please. That would save all this unnecessary…

FATHER DAVIS: Frank…

KATHERINE: *(She does an about face.)* I'm in over my head here.

CARDINAL: The secular world sucked you in big time, Katie.

KATHERINE: It also taught me something.

CARDINAL: To be ashamed of your faith?

FATHER DAVIS: Frank, what are you doing?

CARDINAL: She talks to that deranged boy who tells her you have committed some kind of sin….

KATHERINE: Some kind of crime.

CARDINAL: If it's all untrue, what's the difference?

KATHERINE: You know something?

CARDINAL: Yes. And of which I cannot speak.

KATHERINE: Let me explain to you, Eminence. I'm a reporter. It's my job. I look into things and "report", whether they're earthquakes or human actions.

CARDINAL: But if the earthquake didn't happen and you report it, you'd seem a little crazy wouldn't you?

KATHERINE: So let me confirm that the earth didn't move.

CARDINAL: Is it ethical to pay cash for information?

KATHERINE: It's not the best way but…

CARDINAL: That's prostituted information.

KATHERINE: Even a prostitute can tell the truth.

CARDINAL: Your one flaw was always that you never listened well enough. I told you I can't speak of it. Let it go.

KATHERINE: This is not getting on my good side.

CARDINAL: I DON'T NEED TO GET ON YOUR GOOD SIDE. WHAT'S HAPPENED TO YOU? WHO DO YOU THINK YOU ARE?

(KATHERINE *makes to leave.*)

FATHER DAVIS: Katie. Please. What's the kid's name?

KATHERINE: I can't…give that out.

FATHER DAVIS: Is he the only one making this accusation?

KATHERINE: I've talked to others but…

FATHER DAVIS: There are no others.

KATHERINE: So far, Thank God.

CARDINAL: Oh Thank God? Thank God you know enough to say Thank God.

FATHER DAVIS: Where is he?

KATHERINE: He signed himself into a…well, a psychiatric facility.

CARDINAL: When?

KATHERINE: This morning.

CARDINAL: Didn't he tell you where he was last night?

KATHERINE: Where was he?

CARDINAL: Here. Rosetti saw him. Who is paying for his treatment?

KATHERINE: If he's diagnostically unstable his allegations won't be credible. What's the objection? I don't get it.

CARDINAL: I asked, who is paying for his treatment?

KATHERINE: I am.

CARDINAL: You're a fool.

FATHER DAVIS: Isn't that a little inappropriate?

KATHERINE: I leave those judgements to my employer.

CARDINAL: Does your employer know about it?

KATHERINE: You're ganging up on me and I am out of here.

CARDINAL: No. Wait. I apologize. What was I thinking? I'm a fool. I really am. I'll stay out of it. I think you and Father Davis should have lunch, on me.

FATHER DAVIS: No no, Cardinal.

CARDINAL: You can talk more freely without me around. I have too much at stake and I am too nervous. Have lunch. Have a drink.

KATHERINE: Have him ring me up at the paper.

CARDINAL: Ask him.

KATHERINE: Would you ring me up?

CARDINAL: Answer her. How about today?

KATHERINE: Uhhh. Make it a drink at say five?

CARDINAL: He'll be there.

KATHERINE: You know the Cafe Etoile?

CARDINAL: Yes. He does. The Etoile. Say you'll be there. *(No response)* He'll be there. You better believe he'll be there.

(KATHERINE exits.)

CARDINAL: Is she not the biggest pain in the ass that ever set foot in this rectory? Why didn't you answer her? What is bugging her about you?

FATHER DAVIS: It's so obtuse, I'd rather…

CARDINAL: Obtuse my foot. You have degrees in philosophy and theology. Make a damn stab at it.

FATHER DAVIS: She wrote to me, after her father died, demanding evidence that God exists.

CARDINAL: And you told her?

FATHER DAVIS: It was couched in…well emotional terms. Like would she ever see her father again, in heaven.

CARDINAL: I'm sure he went to heaven. He was a good man. What did you tell her?

FATHER DAVIS: Well I didn't tell her she would see her father again.

CARDINAL: You die in the state of grace, you go to heaven. What did you tell her?

FATHER DAVIS: At the time, people were reading a book based on a series of lectures by a professor at the University of Chicago…

CARDINAL: You sent her a book?

FATHER DAVIS: Yes, I…

CARDINAL: Why not Saint Augustine? Or just tell her heaven exists. Have her read the gospels.

FATHER DAVIS: The idea of a literal heaven is out dated even among some of our own theologians.

CARDINAL: Then send her to another priest if you're confused yourself. Oh Blessed Mother. What did this book say?

FATHER DAVIS: Cardinal…

CARDINAL: What did the book say?

FATHER DAVIS: It presented new possibilities about how to think about our ultimate end, our life on earth, our death.

CARDINAL: What new possibilities? What new possibilities?

FATHER DAVIS: I wrote her a long letter that I…

CARDINAL: WHAT NEW POSSIBILITIES?

FATHER DAVIS: There are other ways of explaining death and happiness, Your Eminence, not just by manufacturing a fantasy.

CARDINAL: What did you just say?

FATHER DAVIS: Frank…

CARDINAL: Is this why you sit in the back and never say mass?

FATHER DAVIS: I don't believe in it.

CARDINAL: You said mass yesterday.

FATHER DAVIS: I tried and shouldn't have.

CARDINAL: Do you not believe in God?

FATHER DAVIS: Don't put me through this, Frank.

CARDINAL: I want you to see a psychiatrist. Get an anti-depressant… You deliberately pulled the rug out from under a Catholic woman, one of my parishioners?

FATHER DAVIS: I wrote her an apology. Weeks went by. I wrote again. Apologized. Anguished. Wrote again and again. She never answered so I called her mother who screamed saying I sent her daughter on a futile philosophical journey and I just gave up.

CARDINAL: So that's it. I am stunned by the sheer lack of judgement…

FATHER DAVIS: Frank…

CARDINAL: Shut up. …of a priest, letting a parishioner in, on his own lack of faith.

FATHER DAVIS: She was a friend.

CARDINAL: She was a lay person. What is faith but belief without evidence?

FATHER DAVIS: I can't make that work.

CARDINAL: Oh Sonny…

FATHER DAVIS: I value the affection by which you call me Sonny, but…

CARDINAL: *(Overlap)* What's this now?

FATHER DAVIS: …I'm not you're son.

CARDINAL: *(Overlap)* It never bothered you.

FATHER DAVIS: I don't want you to get any closer.

CARDINAL: I'm already close.

FATHER DAVIS: I'm trying to prepare you.

CARDINAL: For what?

FATHER DAVIS: Disappointment. I…

CARDINAL: You've already disappointed me.

FATHER DAVIS: You don't know what I've done.

CARDINAL: What are you going to tell me now? Jesus help us. I don't want to know. Listen to me…

FATHER DAVIS: Frank…

CARDINAL: You are going to get this problem with that poor woman out of the way before anything else. You hear me? Nip it.

FATHER DAVIS: Forget her.

CARDINAL: I will not forget her. You insulted her faith and she's offended. Apologize and this time, make her accept it.

FATHER DAVIS: I want to retire.

CARDINAL: You're too young to retire. No. You're going to do this for me.

FATHER DAVIS: I'm going to be in trouble. You're not listening…

CARDINAL: I KNOW I'M NOT LISTENING. YOU THINK I DON'T KNOW WHAT YOU WANT TO TELL ME? I DON'T WANT TO HEAR IT. YOU ARE NOT LISTENING TO ME. We've got a window…

FATHER DAVIS: *(Overlap)* We don't have a win…

CARDINAL: Your faith? That's your business….

FATHER DAVIS: *(Overlap)* It's not about…

CARDINAL: …but the church? That is my business and my God has given you a damn window and you are to pull yourself together. This is making me dizzy.

FATHER DAVIS: Just let me tell you…

CARDINAL: I DON'T WANT YOU TO TELL ME WHAT YOU'VE "DONE". I DON'T WANT TO HEAR YOUR SINS. TELL THEM TO ROSETTI. Oh God, Oh God, Oh God. I thought we were in the clear. This towering corporation, inflate it to monstrous proportions then drop it on the diocese and walk? The trucks, the kitchens, real estate, the banks? No no no. The young man recanted. He lied.

FATHER DAVIS: It won't do us any good.

CARDINAL: You're having a drink with McGuire. Get somewhere with her.

FATHER DAVIS: She doesn't like me.

CARDINAL: "You dislike me, Katie McGuire"? Throw it in her face like a man, apologize and do something to help yourself. Or would you rather slink off like a wimp? I'm...

FATHER DAVIS: *(Overlap)* I'm not a...

CARDINAL: ...sick of men who can't stand up to women.

FATHER DAVIS: I CAN STAND UP TO ANYTHING AND I HAVE ON YOUR ACCOUNT AND ON THE ACCOUNT OF A MILLION KIDS, HOLY MOTHER CHURCH, YOU NAME IT AND YOU KNOW IT.

CARDINAL: Alright-alright.

FATHER DAVIS: The very idea you'd call me a Goddam wimp after all I've accomplished here.

CARDINAL: Let's talk in a calmer...

FATHER DAVIS: How can I? I'm furious.

CARDINAL: The drug I take for my prostate... Hytrin. Makes me dizzy. I can faint. You don't want to see me collapse at your feet. Do you Sonny? I called you Sonny. What am I supposed to call you now? Father? Just don't let Rosetti in on this.

ROSETTI: Don't let Rosetti in on what?

(ROSETTI enters carrying three video cassettes. The CARDINAL makes a remarkable, almost manic recovery.)

CARDINAL: Did you know I was voted most popular in high school?

ROSETTI: I have three movies here...

CARDINAL: Every kid in the neighborhood wanted to get into our "crowd" but we were exclusively devoted to one another. We'd go to the ice cream parlor after Mass and sit ten guys in a booth. I hated Sunday afternoon. Oh the gloom and doom of a Sunday afternoon. Those were the darkest hours of my young soul and… *(He swings to almost weepy sadness.)* Sunday nights were more dreadful than slinking down the River Styx into hell and here we are in the gloom and doom of another Sunday night. But our little crowd stays together in this rectory. We all started out good. When we lay face down, prostrate before God, we were all one, together, in love. We will not go our separate ways. Not if Angelo can help it, Angelino Rosetti, little angel of the little roses…

ROSETTI: Please, your Em…

CARDINAL: …who carries in his hands twenty-first century celluloid candles that curse the darkness. The girl at Blockbuster saves him the videos they keep at the back of the store.

ROSETTI: Opera videos. I got the new print of *Going My Way* with Barry Fitzgerald and Bing Crosby. How things used to be.

CARDINAL: What else do you have there Canio?

ROSETTI: Two animal movies. *Free Willie Three* and *Reservoir Dogs.*

CARDINAL: Give me the *Willie* thing and you watch it with me.

ROSETTI: I've seen it.

CARDINAL: I meant Andrew.

FATHER DAVIS: I… No, I…

CARDINAL: What do you want? The dog movie?

FATHER DAVIS: Neither. I…

CARDINAL: Have you seen either?

FATHER DAVIS: No. I...

CARDINAL: You're not going to let me watch *Free Willie* alone in my room after my depressing panegyric.

FATHER DAVIS: Too much on my mind, Frank.

ROSETTI: Nobody seems to be, ahem..."going your way".

CARDINAL: Am I your buffoon, Angie?

ROSETTI: I was only trying to be...

CARDINAL: You profess a rather cloying asceticism, which mixes sarcasm and benevolence, two inharmonious traits.

(Getting serious now)

ROSETTI: You mustn't judge my spirituality.

CARDINAL: And you'd ridicule me in front of a friend...

ROSETTI: *(Overlap)* It was a joke.

CARDINAL: You hurt me, you Bastard.

ROSETTI: He's my friend too.

CARDINAL: *(To* FATHER DAVIS*)* And you'd watch him humiliate me and not stand up for me?

ROSETTI: I was kidding.

CARDINAL: Let him speak for himself. And quit these passive displays of sarcasm and spit the anger out to my face.

ROSETTI: I keep a veil over it.

CARDINAL: Because you're a coward.

ROSETTI: No one can talk to you.

CARDINAL: Bull shit.

ROSETTI: Oh c'mon. I give you back what I get in kind.

CARDINAL: WELL I AM YOUR SUPERIOR WHETHER YOU LIKE IT OR NOT.

ROSETTI: SUPERIOR IN WHAT? IN WHAT, FRANK? DAMN IT. BE HUMAN. WE ALL ARE DEALING WITH THIS THING.

CARDINAL: I feel things too. I feel a lot if I don't show it.

ROSETTI: Then I'll stop it.

FATHER DAVIS: I apologize, Frank.

CARDINAL: Least said, sooner mended. I'm sorry too. I'm so sorry. *(He walks off.)*

FATHER DAVIS/ROSETTI: Good afternoon, Your Eminence.

(CARDINAL exits)

FATHER DAVIS: Careful.

ROSETTI: You must have told him.

FATHER DAVIS: Not quite. He refused to hear it.

ROSETTI: You should have shouted it at him.

FATHER DAVIS: HOW DO YOU SHOUT IT OUT? IT'S NOT THE KIND OF THING YOU SHOUT. HE KNOWS. I THINK HE KNOWS. HE JUST DOESN'T WANT TO.

ROSETTI: We're burning out here.

FATHER DAVIS: He's scared of what he'll have on his hands.

ROSETTI: There was only one kid? Are you sure?

FATHER DAVIS: Oh don't put me through this again.

ROSETTI: Assure me.

FATHER DAVIS: I told you. There was only one.

ROSETTI: His name again?

FATHER DAVIS: Willie Draper.

ROSETTI: Is he the person accusing you now?

FATHER DAVIS: I don't know. But there was only one who could say it and have it be true. One. I told you. One.

ROSETTI: And he was underage?

FATHER DAVIS: I didn't think of his age.

ROSETTI: What do you think?

FATHER DAVIS: I didn't think about how old he was. He was a young man.

ROSETTI: *(Overlap)* Shhhhhh.

FATHER DAVIS: It was three years ago.

ROSETTI: What happened to your faith?

FATHER DAVIS: That light went out all on it's own.

ROSETTI: Of God?

FATHER DAVIS: I don't think I ever really did believe in…I must have been just hiding, like in a children's story.

ROSETTI: And that led you to that boy? Come on.

FATHER DAVIS: It did. He reminded me of myself.

ROSETTI: Don't try to make it philosophical and pretty.

FATHER DAVIS: I'M IN A STRESSFUL ENVIRONMENT ANGELO, OVERWORKED. FATALISTIC AND SOMEONE COMES ON TO ME THAT WAY…

ROSETTI: THAT'S MORE LIKE IT.

FATHER DAVIS: I SEDUCED HIM, ANYWAY YOU LIKE IT. AM I MAKING LIGHT OF IT? I CONFESSED IT AND NOW YOU'RE HAUNTING ME WITH IT? DO YOU WANT ME TO HATE MYSELF?

ROSETTI: I want you to face yourself.

FATHER DAVIS: I just did. It's you who can't face me.

ROSETTI: I am facing you. I'll protect you with my own life. And that is why I'm telling you now, Walk out of here. Just walk out.

FATHER DAVIS: And go where?

ROSETTI: India. South America.

FATHER DAVIS: God's given us a window. It's what he said.

ROSETTI: His God has a window. You have no God. Don't listen to him. He's treacherous as a fox.

FATHER DAVIS: I loved that kid.

ROSETTI: That is disgusting.

FATHER DAVIS: Angie…

ROSETTI: A man as good as you, saying that you…

FATHER DAVIS: Do you know what it is?

ROSETTI: You're not the tragic hero. You can never be a hero again to anyone.

FATHER DAVIS: You think I don't know that?

ROSETTI: You don't. Listen to you. If you had one damn ounce of faith you could at least believe you were forgiven.

FATHER DAVIS: I don't want it.

ROSETTI: I don't know what to do. I don't know what to do. If I've hurt you by anything I've…

FATHER DAVIS: Don't make me laugh.

ROSETTI: Look I… Why don't you join me? I have a tape of *Tosca*—Act Two with Callas and Gobbi where she sings *Vissi D'Arte* and then stabs him to death.

FATHER DAVIS: I got my orders to have a drink with an old friend.

ROSETTI: You poor fool. You don't know what they plan to do to you.

(ROSETTI *exits.* FATHER DAVIS *moves to where he is meeting* KATHERINE.)

Scene Seven

(*Cafe L'Etoile. Five P M*)
(KATHERINE *is sitting graciously sprawled, like a woman having her portrait painted, legs crossed in a gesture of defiance.*)

FATHER DAVIS: May I?

KATHERINE: Sure. Sit down.

FATHER DAVIS: Hi.

KATHERINE: Hi.

FATHER DAVIS: Why are you giving me those hard eyes? Afraid to know me again?

KATHERINE: Know you again?

FATHER DAVIS: Without prejudice. When you liked me.

KATHERINE: You're not who I thought.

FATHER DAVIS: I was.

KATHERINE: Not anymore.

FATHER DAVIS: Maybe it's you who changed.

KATHERINE: Not the way you did.

FATHER DAVIS: I didn't think you judged. I thought you only reported.
What's the problem? Did I damage your faith? Was I the sole cause? I'm probably damaging it more right now. I don't know what to say.

KATHERINE: Can't blame a girl for idealizing men who's hearts belong to God.

FATHER DAVIS: Baloney. Until Lancelot cheats on you and then you become the dragon lady.

KATHERINE: Make this about me. It'll get you off the hot seat for about two minutes.

FATHER DAVIS: Your marriage is in trouble.

KATHERINE: Okay. It's about me. He's a good man and my daughter thinks I'm a beast, but…

FATHER DAVIS: You're leaving them?

KATHERINE: I talked myself, not very convincingly, into believing that I loved someone and married the guy. Then I met the man who taught me what being in love really is. You don't have the only option on throwing your life away.

FATHER DAVIS: Is that what I did?

KATHERINE: I'm rotten. I know what rotten is.

FATHER DAVIS: If I avoided what's rotten in people I wouldn't be in this business.

KATHERINE: A priest with no God?

FATHER DAVIS: No different than falling out of love.

KATHERINE: Then get a divorce.

FATHER DAVIS: Why don't I?

KATHERINE: Maybe so you could meet kids like Will Draper? If that's too rude, I'm sorry. You did a lot for Will. Gave him the birth record of a boy who was killed…

FATHER DAVIS: He needed protection from his own father.

KATHERINE: His blood father?

FATHER DAVIS: His blood father.

KATHERINE: Protection? What kind of protection?

FATHER DAVIS: My two minutes up already?

KATHERINE: You had him tested for H I V.

FATHER DAVIS: *(Overlap)* Don't...

KATHERINE: He was negative, got him an apartment with Rescue House Funds, even an allowance. No record of your doing this for any other kid.

FATHER DAVIS: Do it all the time, Katie.

KATHERINE: Why's he making trouble?

FATHER DAVIS: Been stalking me a couple of years now.

KATHERINE: He's gay now?

FATHER DAVIS: He tell you he was straight?

(Remaining in her relaxed position with legs crossed, KATHERINE *simply stares at* FATHER DAVIS, *rocking a foot.)*

FATHER DAVIS: What's wrong?

(Now KATHERINE's *smiling to show she is not gullible.)*

FATHER DAVIS: What did I say?

KATHERINE: He told me he is straight. Yes.

FATHER DAVIS: And you believed him?

KATHERINE: He swore up and down.

FATHER DAVIS: Did you grill him?

KATHERINE: Would I do that?

FATHER DAVIS: Yeah. Beware of straight people who swear up and down.

KATHERINE: You should know better.

FATHER DAVIS: So we're not talking about what down with you and me.

KATHERINE: I'm happy to talk it out someday but we're in a time constraint and I'm trying to prevent the downfall of a diocese.

FATHER DAVIS: You're hurting me.

KATHERINE: What am I doing?

FATHER DAVIS: Just by the way you're looking at me.

KATHERINE: Please. Tell me about this kid.

FATHER DAVIS: You're an amateur with a kid like him.

KATHERINE: So be the wise serpent and enlighten me. He stalked you.

FATHER DAVIS: He was in love with me.

(KATHERINE *bolts*.)

FATHER DAVIS: What are you looking at me like that for?

KATHERINE: He was in love with you? How'd you learn that?

FATHER DAVIS: Oh c'mon.

KATHERINE: How'd you find out he was in love with you?

FATHER DAVIS: I was behind him one day, I grabbed his shoulders….

KATHERINE: Why do something like that?

FATHER DAVIS: To relax him. He'd gotten himself in a fight. Bruises. Cuts…

KATHERINE: So you touched him?

FATHER DAVIS: Oh please. On his shoulders to relax him.

KATHERINE: And this makes him gay?

FATHER DAVIS: No. He spun around and held me.

KATHERINE: Did you object?

FATHER DAVIS: No. He was crying, his face pale…and suddenly he blurts out: I'm gay, I can't help it. Don't be mad at me, Father. I'm in love with you.

KATHERINE: So he lied to me that he was straight.

FATHER DAVIS: What difference does it make?

KATHERINE: Because if he's that big a liar how can I believe him, right?

FATHER DAVIS: He'd betray his mother to get off the streets for a night.

KATHERINE: He had thoughts of suicide.

FATHER DAVIS: Just be careful your good intentions don't brand you with a big H right in the middle of your forehead just like it's doing me.

KATHERINE: About the H on your forehead...

FATHER DAVIS: Don't...

KATHERINE: I meant H for honesty.

FATHER DAVIS: I meant H for homophobia which is oozing out of your face right now.

KATHERINE: Fuck you, Father.

FATHER DAVIS: You're surprisingly bitchy for a Buddhist.

KATHERINE: What is that for a priest to say?

FATHER DAVIS: I should have said fuck you back.

KATHERINE: Say it. What are you too good? FUCK ME. SAY IT.

FATHER DAVIS: I think you should tell your boss you have a conflict of interest.

KATHERINE: You think you'll get a better deal?

FATHER DAVIS: You think you know me, Katie.

KATHERINE: No, but I've been studying up on you. There's lots I didn't know. (*She opens her notebook.*) Your father was a cop who ate dinner with his gun on the table. What's that? Your mother complained and he was given a desk job. When you were twelve he enrolled you in the P A L.

FATHER DAVIS: How'd you dig that up?

KATHERINE: …A man named Andrew Fox. Lived next door.

FATHER DAVIS: Mister Fox.

KATHERINE: Became like a big brother. That the idea?

FATHER DAVIS: He taught me to swim and lift weights. What's…?

KATHERINE: He raped a boy and hung himself in prison.

FATHER DAVIS: What? I never heard that.

KATHERINE: If you were a victim…

FATHER DAVIS: *(Overlap)* No way.

KATHERINE: The Cardinal, even Rothenberg wants this to blow away. For my part, I could watch you burn and not blink.

FATHER DAVIS: You must have plenty of proof.

KATHERINE: Instinct. Proof is a different animal but if it's out there I'll nail it.

FATHER DAVIS: To punish me or God?

KATHERINE: Don't do Billy Graham on me.

FATHER DAVIS: I should have lied to you about what I was going through.

KATHERINE: Nonsense, I loved the book. I still read it. And I have a lot of gay friends. I'm no homophobe but I'll admit I bolt putting the word gay before the word priest. And, I'm sorry. I believe the kid and feel no less sorry for you as I do for him.

FATHER DAVIS: You feel sorry for me?

KATHERINE: Did you love him?

FATHER DAVIS: *(Long pause)* Yeah.

KATHERINE: Did you "make" love to him? *(Long pause, looking at her)* What's the matter?

(Longer pause)

(FATHER DAVIS *stands and throws money down on the table.* KATHERINE *tosses it toward him.)*

KATHERINE: I've got it covered.

(FATHER DAVIS *turns to walk.)*

KATHERINE: You're the one tossing out words like love and homophobia but I'm dealing with criminal allegations. What is it? A shell game? I don't want to play a shell game. Why can't you spit it out?

FATHER DAVIS: "All wrapped up over a Bloody Mary, Huh? Neat job, Katie McGuire."

KATHERINE: *(Overlap)* Father…

FATHER DAVIS: I should help you hurt me? Who would do that?

KATHERINE: Someone honest.

FATHER DAVIS: You admit your rottenness, like there's virtue in the lack of virtue, a trick of mine, that I'm ashamed of. You should be as well.

KATHERINE: You keep making it about me.

FATHER DAVIS: It gets addictive, pointing the finger away from yourself. Humanity is disgusting sometimes. *(He gulps down the last of his drink and makes to walk out.)*

KATHERINE: Sit. Andrew. Sit. Wait.

FATHER DAVIS: Can't stand it.

KATHERINE: What? Your immorality, your cowardice? The shame you feel, lying to my face? You want to be friends…

FATHER DAVIS: I may be immoral and ashamed but I'm not a coward and I haven't lied to you, unlike your protege. The kid's got you wrapped around his dirty little finger.

KATHERINE: Don't walk out on me.

Scene Eight

(*Seven P M. Sunday night in the Clinic. T V cartoons are playing on* WILL*'s T V.* WILL *has commandeered a wheel chair and is showing off his moves.*)

WILL: Hey. Watch this.

KATHERINE: Where's your shirt?

WILL: I'm hot. Now watch this…wait, lemme try again.

KATHERINE: I telephoned your father in Colorado.

WILL: What? I gave you distinct orders not to get in touch with my Dad.

KATHERINE: I thought he might help us.

WILL: YOU DIDN'T HAVE MY PERMISSION. I TOLD YOU. EVERYTHING WITH MY PERMISSION.

KATHERINE: That's right. I'm sorry.

WILL: That does it. I can't trust you.

(WILL *uses the T V remote like a weapon, raising the volume then shutting off the T V entirely.*)

KATHERINE: I did it for you.

WILL: Oh baby don't try to get me to swallow that. What for me? What am I gettin' outta this?

KATHERINE: I'd love you to tell me.

WILL: Did my Dad help? He made things worse, didn't he?

KATHERINE: (*Overlap*) Why are you so…?

WILL: Why don't you fuckin' listen to me? I told you all my life my father's made this big thing out of I'm a liar. He's spread the word wherever we lived, whoever I knew…

KATHERINE: Why?

WILL: Now you go to him, he thinks I ratted on him but I didn't did I? I could have told you the whole story.

KATHERINE: What story?

WILL: Oh you know what I'm talkin' about.

KATHERINE: What'd he do?

WILL: FIGURE IT OUT FUCKFACE!

KATHERINE: Will....

WILL: You got me mad. I'm sorry.

KATHERINE: Try to relax, try...

WILL: I've been trying. That's what I've been trying to do.

(KATHERINE *approaches the wheel chair from behind. She touches the* WILL's *shoulder.*)

WILL: What're you doin' now?

KATHERINE: Chill. C'mon.

(KATHERINE wipes back WILL's hair.

WILL: Oh Great!

KATHERINE: If you had your pick, would it be some gal or some dude?

WILL: Some dude? We in a surfer movie? Are you comin' on to me? What's with you?

KATHERINE: You're avoiding the question.

WILL: Oh spit it out.

KATHERINE: How many lies did you tell me, Will? C'mon Babe.

WILL: Look at you. What did my Dad tell you?

KATHERINE: How far would you go with a John?

WILL: Oral's okay. I would even kiss a guy if he paid extra.

KATHERINE: Women you kiss for free?

WILL: Of course. You up for a freebie?

KATHERINE: Now don't play with me.

WILL: Why not? C'mere. My tongue can't lie if it's down your throat.

KATHERINE: We're in the psychiatric unit of a hospital, Will. Aren't you afraid they would see you?

WILL: That's the excitement.

KATHERINE: Okay, I think you had special feelings for Father Davis.

WILL: You callin' me a faggot? C'mon. Say it. Fag.

KATHERINE: I don't use that expression.

WILL: No, but you think that expression.

KATHERINE: Why'd you wait a couple of years to blow the whistle?

WILL: You know everything.

KATHERINE: You had feelings for the priest and he hurt you.

WILL: *(Panic)* I am straight. S-T-R-A...I go with a man? But I don't do it in here, in my heart, okay? I do it for the fuckin money. It's my job. Like you, you're interested in me because... what... information makes you money. But would you make love to a woman? Naaa. Because you're straight. Four Star Generals, all straight, right? All these doctors here, man, what are they? Hey, I'm straight. My father's straight. We got a priest here who hangs out with Dead Boys who's so straight everybody thinks I'm lyin'. Who else is straight? Shit, by now even gay people should be straight. Get lost, man. Outta my sight.

KATHERINE: You never grabbed him and told him you were in...?

WILL: Go to the Combat Zone. Ask for a kid named Chintzy. Ask for Mickey Mouse or Blue Nose. They all know he liked me. There's only one person still thinks he didn't touch me and that's his boss cause I told him not.

KATHERINE: Who's his boss?

WILL: The freakin' Cardinal who do you think? Made him hear my confession, matter of life or death...

KATHERINE: You talked to the Cardinal? No.

WILL: *(Amused)* I went to confession. He's a nice guy. He gave me his rosary beads, his own mother's.

KATHERINE: No kidding. Lemme see. *(Laughs deceitfully)* Wow! You got these out of him?

(WILL puts on the rosary beads like a necklace.)

WILL: Is this cool man? I told him I lied about the sex and he comes up with five hundred bills for me to give to the paper. I got two five hundred dollar payoffs. Can I swing both ways or what?

KATHERINE: You little scum bag.

WILL: What, no more tongue in my mouth?

KATHERINE: You set me up.

WILL: I don't want him that ripped open, okay? I told ya, I'm in charge here and I want his people to stick by him when you spill his guts all over your stupid fuckin' paper.

(KATHERINE provokes WILL.)

KATHERINE: Why? He's a hypocrite. He's a creep.

WILL: Don't call him names.

KATHERINE: A homosexual. A pederast.

WILL: Shut up! It wasn't that.

(KATHERINE, *daring to challenge* WILL's *lies, kneels to him, takes his head in her hands as if to kiss him. He pretends interest then pushes her away. The wheel chair rolls back. She stands.)*

WILL: That doesn't prove nothin'. You had no right.

KATHERINE: You care about him, after all he did to you?

WILL: I told you. *(He cries.)*

KATHERINE: Will…

WILL: So I'm a common fag.

KATHERINE: Don't call yourself that. Get dressed. I'm takin' you out of here.

WILL: Oh no. I signed myself in.

KATHERINE: I'll talk to the social worker. C'mon. I'm dropping you off.

WILL: Where?

KATHERINE: Where ever you're headed.

WILL: WHERE AM I HEADED? They're helping me here. You know I'm a liar. I lied all my life but I told you the truth about him.

KATHERINE: Tell it to this recorder or else this whole deal is off here. This place costs money.

WILL: Turn it on.

(A click as KATHERINE *turns on a tape recorder.)*

WILL: He was giving a talk in Saint Louis and he took me on the trip. This was the first time it happened. There was this like double bed, maybe bigger, I don't know but we had to sleep in it together.

KATHERINE: You had to?

WILL: I…yeah. It was one of those Ramada Inns.

KATHERINE: There was no couch in the room?

WILL: There was a couch.

KATHERINE: Then why…?

WILL: I figured he would tell me to sleep on it but he didn't.

KATHERINE: Why didn't you do it of your own accord?

WILL: I dunno.

KATHERINE: You wanted to sleep with him? *(Beat)* You did.

WILL: Yeah. I wanted to know if…if he…

KATHERINE: Cared for you?

WILL: Yes. Yeah.

KATHERINE: Okay. So what happened?

WILL: Next to him in bed…I could feel the tension, you know?

KATHERINE: What do you mean?

WILL: Like a kinda waitin' for something to happen.

KATHERINE: On who's part?

WILL: His…and mine.

KATHERINE: Okay.

WILL: So with my knee, I just touched his thigh, here. He didn't move. I slid my foot down, touched his foot, didn't move. Then my hand touched his side here. And I kept going like that and he didn't object.

KATHERINE: He didn't object to what?

WILL: Me goin' down on him.

KATHERINE: That bastard!

WILL: Naaa. I taught him a few things after that.. how to kiss, how to face what it is.

KATHERINE: You became lovers?

WILL: Turn it off. You got enough.

KATHERINE: Do they let you have newspapers in this place?

WILL: Why?

KATHERINE: When the time comes, I'll bring you one.

WILL: You want his ass totally to burn, doncha?

KATHERINE: You're confusing me with yourself, Will. You're the one who blew the whistle. Now give me the rosary beads.

WILL: No way.

KATHERINE: I feel sorry for you, Willie. You've been betrayed and raped by people who were supposed to take care of you but now I want you to give me those beads like a good fella, or I will knock you so flat on your ass you won't know what fuckin' day it is. Give me those beads.

(WILL *hands over the beads and starts wheeling off.*)

WILL: You're worse than he is.

KATHERINE: I know you think so. I may be bad, but not like him.

(WILL's *comment shames* KATHERINE. *She exits.*)

Scene Nine

(*Sunday, eleven P M.* ROSETTI *and* FATHER DAVIS *are relaxing, reading the paper.* FATHER DAVIS *has a drink.*)

ROSETTI: What is this? In San Diego, a priest rented a plane and flew it into the sun?

FATHER DAVIS: He was in my kind of trouble.

ROSETTI: You know him?

FATHER DAVIS: I just know.

ROSETTI: Why put him in your shoes?

FATHER DAVIS: A priest flying a single engine plane into the sun, that's close as you could get to being an angel.

ROSETTI: He killed himself.

(The YOUNG PRIEST *comes forward, hands and face blackened with ash.)*

FATHER DAVIS: *(Sarcastic)* He became a heavenly body, you know? Just gotta pay with your life.

ROSETTI: You don't know what he was thinking.

FATHER DAVIS: You risk your life when you believe in fairy tales. You have to go higher and higher till your temples throb and there's no oxygen and you get dizzier and dizzier and if you leave the door open, you can even step on a cloud. You die before you hit the water but it doesn't matter because in that small eternity you're the saint in mid air, with your eyes rolled back, coming to earth from heaven.

ROSETTI: He killed himself. You think people care? It only helps them forget he ever existed. If he stayed alive he'd remain part of the human race, part of them. And they'd have to swallow it.

FATHER DAVIS: In jail, the human race cuts your throat.

ROSETTI: At Saint Theresa's, they miss you.

FATHER DAVIS: You think if I go back my troubles won't follow me?

ROSETTI: Anything's better than here.

FATHER DAVIS: They miss who I was, not who I am.

ROSETTI: Maybe you miss them. Father David looks into the audience as through a window.

FATHER DAVIS: Christ on their crosses with real hair, nail polish wounds, paper flowers? But when a girl greets you at the door, with a candle and a white handkerchief on her head. That's as real as saints get. She takes you to a room where her mother is dying. The shades are down. Pilar? *Es el padre.* Old woman opens her eyes. *(Raspy)* Hello Father. Gonna take me to heaven today Father? Yeah. You and me.

ROSETTI: *(Overlap)* Andrew...

FATHER DAVIS: We'll hit the water together.

ROSETTI: Everything takes faith, Andrew, even just staying alive.

FATHER DAVIS: I'm finding that out.

ROSETTI: Pull yourself together. You have confessions in less than an hour. *(He exits.)*

FATHER DAVIS: What's that in your hand?

YOUNG PRIEST: Gasoline truck hit the guard rail and exploded on the bridge. The guy's wallet.

(FATHER DAVIS hands him the YOUNG PRIEST his drink. The YOUNG PRIEST takes a sip.)

YOUNG PRIEST: Police rang, said he was Catholic and... *(Cries)* He sat there totally charred, all ashes and still breathing. I applied the oils and his skin came off. Cops want me to call his wife and family.

FATHER DAVIS: You feel too much.

YOUNG PRIEST: I'm supposed to.

FATHER DAVIS: At least he had people who loved him.

YOUNG PRIEST: Don't start with me.

FATHER DAVIS: Everyone needs someone.

YOUNG PRIEST: You're depressed.

FATHER DAVIS: You know why? You're not going to keep your vows.

YOUNG PRIEST: You don't know what I'll...

FATHER DAVIS: Isn't my face familiar?

YOUNG PRIEST: Let me go.

FATHER DAVIS: Look at me. Closer. In the eyes. Who do you see Andrew?

YOUNG PRIEST: I'LL NEVER BE YOU. I'LL FIGHT IT. I'LL FIGHT IT WITH ALL MY STRENGTH!

FATHER DAVIS: YOU WON'T WIN.

(The YOUNG PRIEST *slips out of* FATHER DAVIS*'s grasp and exits. The* CARDINAL*, in dressing gown, runs into* ROSETTI*.)*

CARDINAL: Go to him. He's having another nightmare.

Scene Ten

(The next evening in the CARDINAL*'s office.)*

ROSETTI: Don't even think you're getting in to see him.

KATHERINE: It's urgent.

CARDINAL: Katie? Let her in.

*(*ROSETTI *exits.)*

KATHERINE: Bad news Eminence. I'm so sorry.

CARDINAL: Get it over with.

KATHERINE: On this little machine, I have painstaking descriptions of kissing, oral sodomy, sex and love between the boy and Father Davis.

CARDINAL: That was the allegation from the beginning. So what are you telling me?

KATHERINE: Wait a minute...

CARDINAL: Sexual improprieties are the most boring things a priest listens to day in and day out. Suddenly you're "the journalist" as if someone stuck a scepter in your hand and now you want to teach me, as if I didn't know that human nature is ambivalent and chaotic.

KATHERINE: I'm the hustler now and your priest is employee of the month? Uh uh.

CARDINAL: I have a niece who loves to deliver catastrophic news. She'd run to be the first to tell you your sister had a stroke.

KATHERINE: Fine. Let's get rid of freedom of speech altogether.

CARDINAL: Going around shaming people is not my idea of freedom.

KATHERINE: Your people created shame.

CARDINAL: And yours turned it into a business. One virgin a day into the volcano.

KATHERINE: Did you know he was a homosexual?

CARDINAL: Jesus never said anything against homosexuality. It was Paul, long after Jesus died and Paul had a lot of personal problems.

KATHERINE: What is it about the truth that you people can't swallow?

CARDINAL: "He's homosexual". You want me to be the Gestapo and drag every Lesbian out of the convents, give priests a pink triangle, whitewash the Sistene chapel, slash half the religious art of the past two thousand years and put a sledgehammer to the Pieta because of Michelangelo? Compared to them, what have you done for Christianity except criticize and renounce it?

(KATHERINE holds up the CARDINAL's beads.)

KATHERINE: Are these really your mother's rosary beads?

CARDINAL: Where'd you get those?

KATHERINE: He conned you out of five hundred dollars and he's laughing his head off.

(The CARDINAL *falls into a chair.)*

KATHERINE: It's all on this machine. An overnight in Saint Louis, the sex games in bed. We've been implicated in nothing more than a gargantuan lovers quarrel. The boy is using me to shame his lover but the little fool wanted to save him in your eyes so the man can keep his damn job.

CARDINAL: What's it feel like to have a heart attack?

KATHERINE: Oh you're not having chest pains now. Please.

CARDINAL: It's my stomach.

KATHERINE: Tell me if you're faking because I'm too exhausted to go through this.

CARDINAL: I need Mylanta.

KATHERINE: I'll call Rosetti.

CARDINAL: No. Help my church Katherine McGuire.

KATHERINE: I thought that's what I was doing.

CARDINAL: Your father would say not.

KATHERINE: He'd be devastated.

CARDINAL: But not blind to the power in his hands. *(He gets up on his feet.)* You can save the biggest juvenile rescue operation in the history of the world.

KATHERINE: I prepared myself for that argument. Don't try it.

CARDINAL: Expose any priest you like, I'll help you but cripple this one who's guilt is still doubtful as far as I'm concerned and you deliver thousands of kids to legions, salivating to get their hands on them, children he saves from hunger, drugs, disease, death, lost kids, sexually exploited kids.

KATHERINE: He exploited one himself.

CARDINAL: One boy? Forget that confused kid. I'm talking about thousands, girls, boys that he saves from chaos.

KATHERINE: He is the chaos.

CARDINAL: You are far more dangerous to those kids.

KATHERINE: I'm not gonna let this happen to me.

CARDINAL: THIS IS NOT HAPPENING TO YOU!

KATHERINE: IT IS HAPPENING TO ME AND IT'S HAPPENING TO MY CHURCH. MY CHURCH! I didn't say that.

CARDINAL: No. Good. Good. You said it. We'll put out one fire at a time.

KATHERINE: Not we. You.

CARDINAL: Thank God you couldn't become a priest. You'd be hanging sinners by their balls. Go to him. Make a deal.

KATHERINE: I offered him a deal at L'Etoile. He turned it down.

CARDINAL: I should never have talked Rothenberg into…

KATHERINE: Don't tell me you got me this job? Please don't. Oh shit. How humiliating.

CARDINAL: I thought we could help one another.

KATHERINE: How could you be so naive and in such wholesale denial? Do you realize you're sacrificing yourself? For what? He did it. You have your beads in your hand and it's on this tape.

(The CARDINAL *stalls.)*

CARDINAL: Did he tell you how he got these?

KATHERINE: Yeah! In confession where he lied to you.

CARDINAL: He's Catholic.

KATHERINE: Well? So?

CARDINAL: If he could lie to a Cardinal in confession, wouldn't he lie to a little black machine? Who is going to believe a hustler's confession? Get the truth out of the priest, not the kid. If you would have approached him the way a priest would, as a friend, as a counselor a confidant, by now we'd know the truth. But you had to feed that vindictive pride and here you are, waking me up to parade a useless tape before me.

KATHERINE: I'm not parading anything.

CARDINAL: You're not the girl I knew. You're an ice cold woman who ridicules her faith, denounces the cross and abandons her flesh and blood for a lover.

KATHERINE: YOU THROW THAT UP TO ME AT THIS MOMENT?

CARDINAL: Oh I do.

KATHERINE: I AM NOT COLD. I AM HURT. HOW COULD YOU THROW THAT UP TO ME?

CARDINAL: Alright-alright-alright.

KATHERINE: AS IF YOU COULD KNOW WHAT MARRIAGE IS, WHAT LOVE IS, AS IF IT WAS EASY GIVING UP WHAT I DID.

CARDINAL: If a priest of mine had anything to do with your giving up the church then...

KATHERINE: *(Overlap)* He had nothing to do with it....

CARDINAL: ...I apologize for him.

KATHERINE: I don't want your apology. I don't need it.

(ROSETTI *comes into view.*)

CARDINAL: He hears confessions every night between seven and eight.

KATHERINE: So?

CARDINAL: He's hearing now. Quiet.

KATHERINE: I'm not going to confess to him.

CARDINAL: You said you're as qualified as any man to be a priest.

KATHERINE: What are you trying to…?

CARDINAL: If you weren't cold then why…?

KATHERINE: What?

CARDINAL: …why didn't you get anywhere with him?

KATHERINE: Not because I was cold.

CARDINAL: Did you antagonize him? Intimidate him? Why wouldn't he come clean?

KATHERINE: BECAUSE HE DOESN'T WANT ME TO KNOW.

CARDINAL: WHY NOT?

KATHERINE: I AM THE ENEMY.

CARDINAL: Exactly. Exactly.

KATHERINE: Oh no.

CARDINAL: Had you offered him trust, you'd have gotten the proof you're still only guessing at. Take it from the lips of Father Davis then you'll have captured reality. Reality. That's what journalism is all about. Not the game you're playing.

KATHERINE: Failing marks in moral theology, I flunk journalism. I wind up being not merely your bad pupil, I'm a bad woman. Now I discover I was your tool, but too cold to ever be anything that resembles a priest. You even got me the job I am standing here defending, as if it were something I earned. You beat me. I'm a little scandalized, you know, because, I can see you're fully conscious of how cruel you are.

(KATHERINE *exits to upstage.* ROSETTI *comes forward.*)

ROSETTI: Why don't you try being a priest and get rid of him yourself?

CARDINAL: Don't interfere.

ROSETTI: You said you'd die on the cross for him.

CARDINAL: And if he's innocent, I will.

ROSETTI: May I remind you? Christ didn't die for the innocent.

CARDINAL: You deliberately refuse to understand me.

Scene Eleven

(KATHERINE *goes to where* FATHER DAVIS *is hearing confessions.*)

KATHERINE: Father, I've been away from the sacraments a long time.

FATHER DAVIS: Speak up, please?

KATHERINE: I've been away from this sacrament for five or six years.

FATHER DAVIS: Katie…?

KATHERINE: Yes, Father.

FATHER DAVIS: Go to another priest.

KATHERINE: I would like to talk to you under the seal of confession. This is not easy for me on my knees this way.

FATHER DAVIS: Find another priest.

KATHERINE: I confessed a lot to you as a kid. You know everything about me and I'm grateful you haven't thrown it in my face.

FATHER DAVIS: I don't remember.

KATHERINE: If I were a priest, would you trust me?

FATHER DAVIS: You're not a priest. I am. I'm vowed to protect your secrets under pain of death yet you kneel here threatening to publicize my sins to the world. Please.

KATHERINE: Tell me anything and I'll keep it under the seal.

FATHER DAVIS: You're going to hear my confession?

KATHERINE: Whatever you tell me will go to the grave with me. I'll never write about it or breathe it under pain of death. Just as if I were a priest.

FATHER DAVIS: What's the value?

KATHERINE: I'll fight like hell if you say you're innocent.

FATHER DAVIS: If I'm not?

KATHERINE: I'll quit my job and walk away.

FATHER DAVIS: Quite a sacrifice but the point of confession is forgiveness. Did you hear me?

KATHERINE: Well what is forgiveness? Teach me. Does it change the offense? No. Heal the offended? No. Does it turn back time? No. Does it erase the incident? So tell me, how do I forgive?

FATHER DAVIS: By witnessing the person's remorse.

KATHERINE: But the person refuses to admit his sin.

FATHER DAVIS: If I said I had sex with the boy, that you'll believe?

KATHERINE: The truth can only come to light from your mouth.

FATHER DAVIS: But if I say I did not do it, you'll doubt me.

KATHERINE: Can't help it. I…

FATHER DAVIS: If I said I did how would you feel?

KATHERINE: Not surprised.

FATHER DAVIS: Disappointed in me? Katie…

KATHERINE: I loved you. Was in love with you…

FATHER DAVIS: Don't…

KATHERINE: And I hated you.

FATHER DAVIS: *(Overlap)* Not listening…

KATHERINE: …for being unable…

FATHER DAVIS: *(Overlap)* Don't talk.

KATHERINE: …to return it. And now this. Disappointment falls short….

FATHER DAVIS: Betrayal.

KATHERINE: Yeah.

FATHER DAVIS: That is not my fault.

KATHERINE: Still I'm suffering.

FATHER DAVIS: You're suffering? Compared to my hustlers who'd give any part of themselves to any stranger of any gender who'd lift them out of meaninglessness for an hour, you have not suffered, Katie McGuire.

KATHERINE: *(Overlap)* Horrible…

FATHER DAVIS: They will serve you on their knees. On their backs. They offer up their bodies for a hit.

KATHERINE: That's tragic.

FATHER DAVIS: …But if you betray them, they'll get even and that's what you and that kid are doing. And I am so ashamed.

KATHERINE: Of?

FATHER DAVIS: Believing in either of you.

KATHERINE: May I see your stole?

FATHER DAVIS: What do you want to do with my stole?

KATHERINE: Just hold it for a second? Like if I were a priest?

FATHER DAVIS: No.

KATHERINE: I knew you wouldn't accept my help.

(Reluctantly, FATHER DAVIS *removes his confessional stole and hands it over.)*

KATHERINE: What does a priest do? Kiss the little cross on it? Like this? Then what, what do you do, you put it around your neck, like so?

FATHER DAVIS: Katie…

KATHERINE: I'll take whatever you say to the grave if you'll honor me with the truth in this confession.

FATHER DAVIS: What good is the truth to a journalist if she has to take it to the grave?

KATHERINE: I'm no journalist. I've been reduced to a friend who cares.

FATHER DAVIS: I hope you never feel this alone in your life, Katie.

(The YOUNG PRIEST *comes within earshot.)*

KATHERINE: You're not alone now.

FATHER DAVIS: I don't believe you.

KATHERINE: Say something. Say something.

FATHER DAVIS: I suppose you'll think it sacrilegious for a homosexual to say he fell in love with Christ. I never realized that's what it was, until I stopped believing in him. Then everything went dark, Katie, Oh that awful nothingness which swallowed up everything, my Jesus, his blessed mother, all the saints. Just gone. I turned around and there was Will.

KATHERINE: You blame God for Will?

FATHER DAVIS: No God, no sin.

KATHERINE: Why someone like him?

FATHER DAVIS: He was there. He wanted me.

KATHERINE: So, he never lied to me when he said you had sex?

FATHER DAVIS: It wasn't about that. It was about two desperate people having something they could give to one another.

KATHERINE: But you had had sex with him?

FATHER DAVIS: Yes.

KATHERINE: The truth actually has an odor, like the holy air on the top of a sacred mountain. It helps you breathe again. Do you feel better?

FATHER DAVIS: You took the place of a priest. Now take my place tomorrow. Go round up the transvestites, the teenage prostitutes and junkies...

KATHERINE: *(Overlap)* That's not my job.

FATHER DAVIS: ...Test them for H I V. Find their parents, but I warn you....

KATHERINE: *(Overlap)* Father...

FATHER DAVIS: ...they don't want their kids back because they're gay, because they are ill, because they're addicted and damaged and defective.

KATHERINE: *(Overlap)* You're not looking at it.

FATHER DAVIS: and there's a new crop at the bus terminal every morning. You go…

KATHERINE: *(Overlap)* Please…

FATHER DAVIS: …find them before the pimps and crackheads find them. Give them soup and sandwiches. You hide them. *(Silence)* Are you there?

(The YOUNG PRIEST *comes into the light.* KATHERINE *is walking off.)*

FATHER DAVIS: KATIE? WHERE ARE YOU GOING? KATIE?

*(*KATHERINE *continues walking away from* FATHER DAVIS *and shouts out as she goes. The* YOUNG PRIEST *moves forward.)*

*(*KATHERINE *exits.)*

Scene Twelve

YOUNG PRIEST: You threw away your life? Why?

FATHER DAVIS: Ask Christ. He became human.

YOUNG PRIEST: Shut up.

FATHER DAVIS: You forget where you came from.

YOUNG PRIEST: We have different memories.

FATHER DAVIS: A bad little kid who thought God's grace would make him over.

YOUNG PRIEST: We are different.

FATHER DAVIS: Bad little kid who walks around like some self appointed little saint.

YOUNG PRIEST: I never lost faith. You did.

*(*FATHER DAVIS *holds the* YOUNG PRIEST *by the wrist. The* YOUNG PRIEST *slips away.)*

FATHER DAVIS: What? Voices in your head. Conversations with the dead.

YOUNG PRIEST: You're a monster. Don't try anything with me.

FATHER DAVIS: Come here. I just want to…

YOUNG PRIEST: I don't trust you.

FATHER DAVIS: I can help you be free. Just let me…

(FATHER DAVIS *catches the* YOUNG PRIEST *by the arm.*)

YOUNG PRIEST: What are you trying to do?

FATHER DAVIS: Come sit.

YOUNG PRIEST: Let me go. I don't want you. I want God. The Blessed Mother. Anyone but you.

FATHER DAVIS: I'm the only one who can help you.

(*The* YOUNG PRIEST *gets free.*)

YOUNG PRIEST: No. I'll die a good priest. You devil.

FATHER DAVIS: How can you die a good priest? How can you die a good priest?

YOUNG PRIEST: YOU'RE NOT DEAD YET.

FATHER DAVIS: Ha ha ha…

YOUNG PRIEST: You're not dead yet. You have time to do a lot for yourself.

FATHER DAVIS: That was smart, very clever. Time to do what?

YOUNG PRIEST: To repent and be saved. I can save you. You see, I can save you.

FATHER DAVIS: How can you save me?

YOUNG PRIEST: Give me your hand.

(*The* YOUNG PRIEST *grabs* FATHER DAVIS'*s hand and places it on the* YOUNG PRIEST'*s chest.*)

YOUNG PRIEST: Feel this heart…

FATHER DAVIS: *(Overlap)* It's dead.

YOUNG PRIEST: You lie. It's alive. Feel it. You feel it? It's on fire with the love of Christ.

(FATHER DAVIS grabs the YOUNG PRIEST's hand and places it on FATHER DAVIS's chest.)

FATHER DAVIS: Now you feel this heart, cold, lied to, abandoned, alone, dying, betrayed.

YOUNG PRIEST: Who? Who betrayed you. Not God.

FATHER DAVIS: You. *(He sings.)* Silent Dad, Silent house. Gun on the table…

YOUNG PRIEST: I don't know what you're…

FATHER DAVIS: Mister Fox?

YOUNG PRIEST: Never heard of him.

FATHER DAVIS: Mother has a migraine. Older brother won't talk. Dad's in the cellar all day and night.

YOUNG PRIEST: Not me.

FATHER DAVIS: Oil truck's pumping oil into Mister Fox's house next door. November. Older boys play cards around his table…

YOUNG PRIEST: Don't remember.

FATHER DAVIS: …but the old Fox is not there, is he? You see one boy at a time going upstairs, passing the window on the landing. One comes down, the other goes up. Where do they go after the landing?

YOUNG PRIEST: I don't want to…

FATHER DAVIS: To the attic to look at his pornography.

YOUNG PRIEST: Gettin' outta here.

(YOUNG PRIEST runs. FATHER DAVIS catches him and wrestles with him physically. The YOUNG PRIEST fights back but is being over come.)

FATHER DAVIS: You ring his bell. You're only thirteen....

YOUNG PRIEST: No. Not listening.

FATHER DAVIS: ...to stand naked before a man your father's age who kneels before you...

YOUNG PRIEST: Don't say it—don't say it.

FATHER DAVIS: You look down at him through clouds, your head's as high as the sun. Now the boy is a king.

YOUNG PRIEST: No. No.

FATHER DAVIS: You ring his bell the next day, and the next day and day after day...

(FATHER DAVIS *has the* YOUNG PRIEST *in his grasp.*)

YOUNG PRIEST: I did penance.

FATHER DAVIS: What did it get you?

YOUNG PRIEST: God. It got me the universe.

FATHER DAVIS: Rocks. You mean rocks in the sky that don't add up to one human brain?

YOUNG PRIEST: And God is in my brain.

FATHER DAVIS: It's all imagined, Andrew.

YOUNG PRIEST: So what if it is? We have to give hope. Someone has to.

(FATHER DAVIS *lifts the* YOUNG PRIEST *and throws him to sit on the bench.*)

FATHER DAVIS: Let people find their own hope. Do something for yourself.

YOUNG PRIEST: I am doing it. Let me go. This is what I want.

FATHER DAVIS: It'll come to an end.

YOUNG PRIEST: I'll end with it. I don't care.

FATHER DAVIS: You'll become me. You'll become me.

(The YOUNG PRIEST *starts to sob helplessly.* FATHER DAVIS *picks him up from behind and throws him down straddling the bench behind him like two men on a horse.)*

YOUNG PRIEST: Don't hurt me.

FATHER DAVIS: I'm gonna help you.

YOUNG PRIEST: What do you want to…?

FATHER DAVIS: I want you to…

YOUNG PRIEST: Don't touch me.

FATHER DAVIS: Go to another city. Get a job.

YOUNG PRIEST: What're you trying to…?

FATHER DAVIS: We can play a trick on time….

YOUNG PRIEST: No. Pray. Pray. Father, who art in heaven, hallowed…hallowed be…thy…what are you doing?

*(*FATHER DAVIS *starts opening the top snaps on the* YOUNG PRIEST*'s cassock.)*

FATHER DAVIS: Shhhhh-shhh-shhh-shhh-shhhhhh.

*(*FATHER DAVIS *slips his hand inside the* YOUNG PRIEST*'s cassock. The* YOUNG PRIEST *leans back to push him away but traps himself deeper into* FATHER DAVIS*'s embrace.)*

YOUNG PRIEST: No. No. Hail Holy Queen mother of mercy…

FATHER DAVIS: Let me touch you.

YOUNG PRIEST: To thee do we cry poor banished children of Eve…

FATHER DAVIS: Please… *(Let me…)*

*(*FATHER DAVIS *grasps the shoulder fabric of the* YOUNG PRIEST*'s cassock.)*

YOUNG PRIEST: Please… Let me go.

FATHER DAVIS: Please… *(Give in to your body)*

YOUNG PRIEST: Please... *(Yeah. Like that)*

FATHER DAVIS: Please... *(Let me go further)*

YOUNG PRIEST: Please, PLEASE... *(Orgasmic)*

FATHER DAVIS: PLEASE.

(A shimmering sound as the YOUNG PRIEST *bolts through the snaps of his cassock and emerges, like a butterfly from its cocoon, a naked* WILL. FATHER DAVIS *is left grasping an empty cassock.)*

WILL: So? You feel better now? Nothing to be ashamed of. Like being married. Makes me wanna...makes me wanna call you, like, I'm ashamed to say it...

*(*WILL *embraces* FATHER DAVIS *from behind. He curls about him like a snake.)*

WILL: Daaaarling. Always wanted to use that word. You passed out in ecstasy? What's the story? Talk to me. Shit. *(Sing song, cajoling)* Whatsamatta? You saaaad? *(Kisses his ear)* Hey, Father. It's your pal Willie. *(Scared)* Say I love you again. I won't let you go. Say it. Say it for me. Why not? You're mean.

FATHER DAVIS: I love you.

WILL: Good. Take a drag. Go ahead.

FATHER DAVIS: No thanks.

WILL: How about a foot rub?

FATHER DAVIS: You're a good kid...

*(*WILL *jumps into his jeans, removes a money clip from a pocket.)*

WILL: I'll go get you some coffee—black with sugar.

FATHER DAVIS: Do me a favor and...

WILL: Look what I got for you. A money clip. Solid silver.

FATHER DAVIS: Where'd you get that?

WILL: Bought it in a store. Not really.

FATHER DAVIS: Go for a walk.

WILL: You always make me feel guilty after.

FATHER DAVIS: You helped me, a lot. You believe me?

WILL: I know it.

FATHER DAVIS: Now I have to tell you something.

(WILL sees it coming.)

WILL: Uh uh. *(No)*

FATHER DAVIS: Can't do this any more. Can't see you.

WILL: *(Panicking)* What'ya think I do it for?

FATHER DAVIS: *(Overlap)* Shhhh, now don't…

WILL: I didn't put out for you to tell me I'm some devil.

FATHER DAVIS: I can't say mass.

WILL: Because of me?

FATHER DAVIS: I lose my state of grace whenever I consent to this.

WILL: You're the one I do it for. It ain't for me.

FATHER DAVIS: Good then. You won't miss it.

WILL: No.

FATHER DAVIS: If you cared about me you would help me stop.

WILL: We can stop. No more. No more.

FATHER DAVIS: You can't come around again.

WILL: Don't tell me that. No. Please, Father. I'm beggin' ya, I'm beggin' ya. Don't do that to me. I really love ya, really love ya.

FATHER DAVIS: My life doesn't allow this.

WILL: Then leave it. It's makin' ya sick anyway. I'll support ya. Sure. I'll be a waiter. *Maitre De.* Pastry Chef. I'll go to cooking school. Chefs make money.

FATHER DAVIS: I am no good.

WILL: I'm good for the two of us.

FATHER DAVIS: You don't know.

WILL: You don't know. I would work. I would be faithful. I would never leave you, never, never, never. We'll get wedding bands.

(FATHER DAVIS *laughs lovingly but it inflames* WILL's *panic.*)

WILL: DON'T LAUGH AT ME!

FATHER DAVIS: You worry me.

WILL: I was never willing to give up so much for anyone in my life as I am for you.

FATHER DAVIS: You sweet kid, what'll you be giving up? It's I who'll be giving up my work, God.

WILL: Well I can't be God. So what do I get for my trouble?

FATHER DAVIS: Now don't try to hurt me.

WILL: I thought you were more than just some John. I wind up with nothing from them, nothing from you. What does that make you? Any different from them?

FATHER DAVIS: Yes. Because I loved you.

WILL: Like it's past tense? So where does it leave me now? I'm shit again.

FATHER DAVIS: Oh, c'mon.

WILL: What is it with you educated people? You go for little broken down guys like me then dump us because we ain't good enough, we ain't old enough, we ain't smart enough.

FATHER DAVIS: Not true.

WILL: Why don't you go after people you'd be willing to give up your life for?

FATHER DAVIS: I already gave up my life.

WILL: Oh, to God. *(He opens his arms and screams to heaven.)* HEY GOD. HE JUST CHEATED ON YOU AGAIN. It'd be different if I was some college graduate.

FATHER DAVIS: I'd have to do this with anyone.

WILL: Do what? Do what? You said you loved me. "I love you." You said it twice…

FATHER DAVIS: I abused you.

WILL: Posh. I was after you from the minute I saw you.

FATHER DAVIS: Well I can't see you anymore.

WILL: 'Cause I'm your sin? That's all I been to you? Your sin boy? *(He grabs the T V remote as if it were a gun.)*

FATHER DAVIS: Willie go for a walk.

WILL: I would have died for you. Killed for you. *(He points the remote.)* You fuck! YOU FUUUUUKKKK!

(And zaps FATHER DAVIS into invisibility. Blackout except for the green television beam that strikes WILL's body. He remains frozen there in that green light. A light on ROSETTI asleep in a chair. His opera video is playing Tosca *very low in volume. The little dinner bell starts ringing on it's own quite madly. In frustration, the bell actually speaks:)*

THE DINNER BELL V O: Angelino, Angelino, Angelino. Little angel of the little roses. Wake up, Angelino, wake up, wake up, wake up. Terrible, terrible, terrible. terrible. The sky just fell!

(ROSETTI wakes up. The voice of a news anchor comes out of the greenish television beam. WILL runs off.)

ANCHOR V O: The charismatic Catholic priest, Reverend Andrew Davis, founder and C E O of Rescue House is being accused this morning of misconduct with a young man who was under age at the time and under the priest's care, according to a feature exclusive by Independent reporter Katherine McGuire.

(Final section of the aria Vissi D'Arte *starts a low crawl in here)*

ANCHOR V O: William Draper, Alias Arthur Washburn Junior is to hold a press conference sometime this morning and sources say that he will confirm the allegation that Father Davis lured him into indecent acts for a period of over a year.

(The aria is now playing in the rectory. The soprano's voice rises in full volume, out over the audience. At the crescendo, a light comes up on ROSETTI *nervously reading a newspaper. A light comes up on the* YOUNG PRIEST *holding the stiletto letter opener.* ROSETTI *shakily pours a brandy and drinks. The* YOUNG PRIEST *slices down his eyelids and across the veins of his neck with the stiletto.* ROSETTI *senses the violence and backs away to exit. Slow blackout on the* YOUNG PRIEST. *As the aria concludes, the* CARDINAL *enters and picks up the newspaper which* ROSETTI *dropped. Tuesday Morning now.)*

Scene Thirteen

*(*FATHER DAVIS *approaches the* CARDINAL.*)*

FATHER DAVIS: Frank...

CARDINAL: Go down to that crowd on the rectory steps and explain it to them.

(The CARDINAL *removes the large cross from his cincture and holds it before* FATHER DAVIS.*)*

CARDINAL: Touch this cross...

FATHER DAVIS: *(Overlap)* Let me talk to…

CARDINAL: …and swear on Christ you did not touch that boy.

FATHER DAVIS: I touched him. You think Jesus doesn't understand my guilt? All those innocents slaughtered because of him…I'm sure he didn't like himself for that.

CARDINAL: Give me that collar.

(The CARDINAL *rips the collar off* FATHER DAVIS's *neck and strikes him.* FATHER DAVIS *steps back and falls.)*

CARDINAL: You made a disgrace of yourself and an animal out of me.

FATHER DAVIS: *(Laughs genuinely)* Ha ha ha ha ha…

CARDINAL: What are you laughing at, you fool?

FATHER DAVIS: Trying to make me believe you're shocked? You can be honest with me Frank. Look at me. I've come to my end. I may even have to kill myself.

CARDINAL: It was rape. He was sixteen.

FATHER DAVIS: I cared for him.

CARDINAL: You'd prefer to call it something else, I'm sure.

FATHER DAVIS: Well, you always wanted to know me.

CARDINAL: The mother of that boy. I am standing her right there…what do you say to her?

FATHER DAVIS: Don't play this game.

CARDINAL: She wants to know how you "cared" for her son. Tell her. Did you penetrate him, make him perform fellatio on you? Tell her what you did with her child.

FATHER DAVIS: Stop calling him a child.

CARDINAL: He was under age at the time. His father was a monstrosity. He was already destroyed, damaged, his pump primed for abuse…

FATHER DAVIS: I AM NOT DENYING IT.

CARDINAL: Lower your voice. Losing your faith as an excuse. No no no. You don't fool me.

FATHER DAVIS: I wasn't trying…

CARDINAL: Saints have lost their faith. It didn't drive them to lechery.

FATHER DAVIS: You go down to them and explain how you tried to outwit them. Go down, Frank. Tell 'em you had no idea what was going on. Lie your head off. I'll back you up.

CARDINAL: I blame myself for whatever wrongs you accuse me of but now you blame yourself for what you've done. Not your faith or lack of it. Not God or the lack of God. YOUR SELF! LET ME HEAR YOU. BLAME YOURSELF.

FATHER DAVIS: Okay. I blame myself.

CARDINAL: Look at me. I'm shaking. I'm so scared. Scared. Hopes, hopes. So many hopes crashed. What you've done to me. You Judas. You Judas. Oh Sonny. Hold me.

FATHER DAVIS: What?

CARDINAL: Everything's going white. Quick. I'm passing out.

FATHER DAVIS: Sit. Here… Sit. You can sit.

CARDINAL: You don't care what happens to me.

(FATHER DAVIS *helps the* CARDINAL *to sit.*)

FATHER DAVIS: Put your head down.

CARDINAL: No.

FATHER DAVIS: Let the blood go… Just stay down. It's your medication. I'll get water.

CARDINAL: What time is it? I'm supposed to say mass. I want you to call the police. I don't want to talk to them.

FATHER DAVIS: You want me…?

CARDINAL: Go pack and leave through the garage. Take a cab to a police station. It's bad for them to show up here. They take pictures. It's too trying…

FATHER DAVIS: I'll do it.

CARDINAL: Be a man.

FATHER DAVIS: Getting you some water.

CARDINAL: No no. Just leave me alone, just pack and… and…go.

FATHER DAVIS: Are you sure you're okay?

(FATHER DAVIS *starts to exit. The* CARDINAL, *like a parent to a child:*)

CARDINAL: Yes, where are you going?

FATHER DAVIS: Frank, I'm going to my room like you…

CARDINAL: To do what there?

FATHER DAVIS: I'm gonna pack, call a cab and go to the police…

CARDINAL: Good boy. Are you feeling better?

FATHER DAVIS: You're kidding.

CARDINAL: Of course not. 'Course not.

FATHER DAVIS: My collar.

CARDINAL: No. No.

(FATHER DAVIS *exits. The* CARDINAL *kneels in prayer, still holding* FATHER DAVIS'*s collar.*)

Scene Fourteen

(KATHERINE *enters. The* CARDINAL *stands.*)

CARDINAL: You can roll your printing presses down the middle aisle. You're the church now. How did you get by Rosetti? ROOOSETTTTTIIII! WHERE ARE YOU? Just look at how cool you are in your immunity. Can you imagine what he's feeling right now?

KATHERINE: He's humiliated. We're all humiliated.

CARDINAL: Thanks to you.

KATHERINE: Thanks to him.

CARDINAL: Now you pay the bill.

KATHERINE: All those hard working people who built this place, like my father who gave you their sweat from the cradle to the grave, they'll pick up the tab, won't they?

CARDINAL: Out. You get out. This is my house.

KATHERINE: Don't do that.

CARDINAL: COVER UP YOUR CRUCIFIXES PEOPLE. SHE'S HEADED YOUR WAY. HIDE YOUR FRAILTY, YOUR SINS, LEST YOU BE SPIT UPON.

KATHERINE: Who's on that cross, Cardinal? A child whom Joseph and Mary cared for as God.

CARDINAL: Who's caring for your kid right now? What do you know of suffering? That cross is the true mystery of life. Love itself is pain. Go to your new sex partner.

(KATHERINE *tries to hold onto the* CARDINAL.)

KATHERINE: Please. You've got to realize that about this I was right.

CARDINAL: I am sick of what is "right". Take your hands off me. The security cameras are watching.

KATHERINE: He broke the law.

CARDINAL: Go to your daughter.

KATHERINE: Don't curse my happiness.

CARDINAL: What do you want, a blessing? Here's your blessing.

(KATHERINE *accepts* FATHER DAVIS's *collar and stares at it.*)

(ROSETTI *appears upstage, dressed in lay clothes. He quietly puts down a suitcase and waits out of their sight.*)

KATHERINE: You people...for the second time...have broken... (*She is too emotional to finish. She just turns and starts to leave.*)

CARDINAL: What? Your heart? Say it. "You people have broken my heart." As if you could be moved.

KATHERINE: And now, you're disowning me again? For what?

CARDINAL: You did it to yourself the first time. Now I'm doing it to you. Get out. I said it before and I meant it. Get the hell outta here. You stink.

KATHERINE: How sad. How unspeakably sad you have made me.

(KATHERINE *throws the collar at the* CARDINAL's *feet and exits.*)

(*The* CARDINAL *tries to pick up the collar but grows dizzy, straightens up quick. He walks to the Cathedra seat and falls into it facing the house.* ROSETTI *comes forward with the dinner bell in one hand, his suitcase in the other. He puts the suitcase down and rings the little bell.*)

CARDINAL: Good idea you're going with him. Knock it off with that bell.

ROSETTI: No one can go with him where he's going.

CARDINAL: Where is he?

ROSETTI: Packing. In his room.

CARDINAL: How does he seem?

ROSETTI: Almost beatific. Radiant in fact.

CARDINAL: I can't imagine that.

ROSETTI: I am telling you the truth.

CARDINAL: So, where are you going?

ROSETTI: I'm retiring, to my own recognizance.

CARDINAL: You mean you're walking out without a dispensation?

ROSETTI: Takes too long. I'm old and I need to discover what it was I gave my life to.

CARDINAL: You don't know?

ROSETTI: This close to the top, it befuddles a lowly priest.

CARDINAL: You should have been closer. Where were you at three every morning? Asleep. Not me. I wake up. I take my pee and my baby aspirin and sit in a chair in the dark. I turn on the T V for company but it catches up to you anyway, what you don't want to know, what you can't bear to know and you sit there until Mass when the people show up and that's the only thing that reminds you what you are and why you belong here.

ROSETTI: Your dinner bell.

CARDINAL: Don't, do this Angelo.

ROSETTI: Take it, Frank. And pray for him.

CARDINAL: I'll pray for you.

ROSETTI: No. Just him.

(ROSETTI *hands over the dinner bell which the* CARDINAL *accepts.*)

CARDINAL: Never forget, Angelo, Thou art a priest forever.

(ROSETTI *looks around for a moment and exits. The* CARDINAL *falls into his Cathedra seat.* FATHER DAVIS *appears high above and behind the* CARDINAL, *presumably in his room. He puts his gun to his head and pulls the trigger. Lights blackout on* FATHER DAVIS. *The* CARDINAL *stands in shock, drops the little bell to the floor. At that instant the great cathedral bell rings for his mass slowly, one, two, then many bells start ringing, madly.)*

(Blackout. The bell ringing ceases, echoes and dies out. Music)

END OF PLAY